POEMS, PRAYERS AND PROMISES

UTSAV JAIN

ISBN 979-888521768-2

Contents

Contents

For every single person who chooses to read this;

Thank you. I would not be a poet without you.

"I hear the soothing lull of sleep
calling me to lands of dreams,
so I pack my bags and bid adieu
and drift off slow, then dive in deep."

Introduction And Acknowledgements

Every single poem ever written is always, in its heart, written with the feeling of love in mind; and if it isn't about the people that inspired them, then the poet himself exists in those words, hiding somewhere only he knows how. Poems do not have to make sense to everyone, not everyone has to relate to every single one of the lines you compose. Poems are supposed to be much more than that. Poetry is about expression, of love, of life, of this world of lies and strife. Even if one person in a distant corner of the world finds solace in the words you pen, in a single poem; then you, as a writer, a poet and a creationist, have come one step close to fulfilling your purpose in this world. That is what I believe anyway. My words are mine, but because you read them, they are yours too. And because they are yours too, they are open to interpretations any way you deem fit. Such is the comfort and freedom of poetry.

People inspire each other more than they would care to admit these days. This life makes us interact with a million different people some way or the other. Some of these people we see and talk to every day; while there are people who have passed us by without us ever taking notice. Make no mistake, even their passing is participation in its own way. There is a handful of people I would like to call out here for their support, inspiration, and validation, this would not have been possible without them.

Shampa Jain – mother – for tolerating my existence for 25 odd years and for being my pillar of support through all the ventures I have ever set forth on.

Aditi Bhaumik – niece – for showering me with validation every single day, and tolerating my 'Hey I wrote something, read it and review it right now.' You are truly one of a kind.

Deep Guha – author, friend – for giving me the occasional and much-needed reality checks.

A special thanks to Jenny Griglani – author, friend – without whose inspiration I never would have found the courage to publish myself.

This book would not have been possible without all the people ever that were in my life, people who were always excited to see me excel, try new things and create art. There is a place for each one of you in my world of words. I thank you, and hope you stay.

Lastly, my unnamed muses and inspirations; thank you for teaching me the many meanings of love and life. I would never have been able to shape my thoughts and feelings into words if it wasn't you. You breathe life into the words I write, for you are the very ink that flows through my veins!

Thank you!

Utsav Jain

21.11.21

1. Little Things

Little smiles that curl on your lips,
Little talks among the both of us.
Little did we know where it all led,
Little did we care for it, too.
Little things remain now,
Little things that were life's worth.
Little things about you,
Little things that went astray.
Little things that led to bigger ones,
Little things that meant much more.
Little things that made it 'Love',
Little things that turned to hate.
Little things called differences.
Little did we spent apart,
Little now we meet.
Little things, it's them,
Little things that fall apart.

2. The Sennight

A sennight we haven't met,
A sennight spent without her presence,
A sennight since we last said goodbye,
A sennight since I last felt her touch.

I miss her,
Like the trees miss the sun by night,
Like the bees miss the flowers of the day,
Like a choking man misses the air.

I long for her,
Like an addict longs his addiction,
Like the dry earth longs for rain,
Like the sky longs for rainbows.

I love her,
But words fail if I ever compare,
My love with any other existence, for
Words were never forged for this.

A sennight we haven't talked,
A sennight I missed her presence,
A sennight I longed for her touch,
A sennight I wished she was here.

I stare at the empty parchment,
A sennight I haven't slept,
But often I wonder, was it
a sennight? Or only yesterday?

3. A letter to the beloved

I know not if you wait,
My beloved;
I wonder with glazed stares.
My soul burns, as
I try to glimpse the pain
That you have endured.

So different, and yet,
So alike are we;
Two children of the sun.
I wish to apologize,
To make you forget your pain,
But vainly struggle for a voice.

How have you been so silent?
How did you ever pass,
Those endless wintry nights?
What's the price, I wonder, for
The thousand-score tears?
I would repay it in blood if I could.

I wish you know,
How much I repent, but
Aimless are my verses, all my words.
How could I have been so cruel?
I often wonder, but.
The answer eludes me.

Let the winds be my messengers,
And carry on this song,
To tell her at last, I'm coming back home.
I hope the doors are ajar,
Like they always used to be,
Waiting for my return.

Forgive me, oh beloved!
For I know not my own life,
Without your magic presence.
Let then Aphrodite smile,
Bestow her grace on me perhaps;
For I wish to return.

I wish to see your smile again,
Nestled in my arms, like,
You always used to be.
Heavens know it is true,
The wrongs I have done,
I never meant to do.

Let then the flowers grow anew,
Let our black roses rejoice,
For now I finally return.
From barren, broken lands I come,
Longing for your soft smile,
And a gentle caress.

I fear the doors have been closed,
The bird has left its cage,
All I have is hope.
Hope guides me, through
These treacherous trenches,
Those familiar strange roads.

I hope you take me back,
Forgive my sins of distance,
And we begin our tale anew.
I know not if you wait,
My beloved!
But hope that you still do.

4. For you, forever

In the sunset sweeping through,
I have waited years for you.
In the aimless streets countless,
I have laughed and cried with you.
In the hues of mornings, dreaming,
I have spent all my hours for you.
On the roofs of ageless buildings,
I have loved and longed for you.
In the night of the starless skies,
I have counted diamonds with you.
In the early hours of winter dawns,
Cold, I have found warmth in you.
In the fiery summer dusks,
On your soul, I have kissed you.
In the crowds of a hundred men,
Breathless, I have once lost you.
In the air swirl clouds of dust,
Amid them again I found you.
In the shops of plastic roses,
I have dreamed of petals for you.
In your eyes like midnight skies,
I have hunted demons for you.

In your crystal tears of pain,
I have fought your sorrows for you.
In the age of fading memories,
I have written poems for you.
In the days of drunken stupors,
I have dreamed of a life with you.
In the horizon of heaven and earth,
I have searched for rainbows for you.
But then, in the real world of lies,
I have dug our graves for you.
And when you were here no more,
I have haunted streets searching for you.
In the eyes of scared children,
I have searched for dreams for you.
In your memories of golden days,
I have spent days daydreaming for you.
And only then did I realize at last,
That I have lived and died for you.

5. Midnight Lullaby

Sleep princess, and,
Let dreams take you far,
Where none but you can roam,
On clouds around the universe,
See galaxies and stars above you,
Glance the world at your feet,
Let joys in your heart awaken,
Sleep princess, sleep.

Sleep angel, and,
By the hours of the darkness,
Forget the hurts amid the sun,
May oblivion be the bane of grief,
You travel on and on and then,
Nestle in his loving arms,
Dream of your One beloved,
Sleep angel, sleep.

Sleep sorceress, and,
Cast myriad spells of bliss,
On yourself, and all around,
Till nothing but joy remains,

Open up your mind now,
And inhale the worldly soul,
Imagine, create, dream and smile,
Sleep sorceress, sleep.

Sleep sister, and
Let nature over you,
Spread its calming pall,
With threads of innocence yours,
Fill the whole world with hope,
And soar away afar,
Dream of an endless horizon,
Sleep sister, sleep.

Sleep beloved, and
With the sweetest dreams,
That cushion your heart,
Dream of tomorrow, today;
When the darkness grows thin,
wake up to joyous beginnings,
and sing a heavenly hymn,
sleep beloved, sleep.

6. Dream a little dream of mine

Dream a little dream of mine,
Where up is upside down,
And we walk among the stars.
Where the world is bigger -
Brighter than the Sun,
And the journey is endless,
With twists and turns so subtle.
Look inside your soul to find this;
Dream a little dream of mine.

Love the way your heart desires,
Be a bird and fly sky high,
Close your eyes and feel alive,
Dream a little dream of mine.

See the horizons stretch afar,
Fall down, get up, and fall again,
Laugh until your stomach hurts,
Dream a little dream of mine.

And when one journey's over,
With another set to begin;
Fall back on your graceful steps,
And come home for the night.
With your eyelids heavy, tired,
Rest under the cloudless canvas,
Sleep, smile, dream,
Dream a little dream of mine.

7. Untitled #1

Dear me darling!
Do you see the time?
We must go at once,
For the world might perceive,
And read between the layers,
To chance out our truths.

Look here now;
The winds run past us,
Silent as hungry serpents -
Slithering, twisting, turning;
And the clouds in the sky
Hide the moonlight pale,
Out of raw juice of shame.
And yet the culprit peeps -
Through the daze of midnight.
Now here we stand together,
Miles apart, and yet close;
Watching the same old crescent,
In all its glorious beauty.
We do not feel so distant anymore,
As our voices echo around,

And our restless minds wonder
Why the stars play games,
Watching us all run about,
On our quests set by them.
Look there dear;
The stars shine now,
And the clouds have gone away;
But they now cloud our judgements,
And refuse to let us sleep.
Do we know what lies ahead?
Can we make it through?
I wish we can, you see -
For it is a beautiful thought
To be together, as one;
With some glances stolen,
Silent smiles and matched gazes,
Some whispered vows,
And sleeplessness.

With an embrace utter gentle,
And a soft kiss goodnight,
Let's try to rise anew tomorrow,
With your arms around my soul,
To survive the mess we've made.

8. Unrequited

I cannot deny you my affections,
hence I deny you my presence.
For my absence will not be felt
Around the many you call friends,
For they deny you of me -
Despite my best efforts.
All your dreams denied, forsaken,
You pack your bags and walk out;
And all I have left is then but,
A mere presence of absence,
That echoes in little dust trails,
Around your naked footfalls aground,
Upon which no new dust settles -
For I have kept it that way,
In denial of your departure.
A helpless mess behind to share,
My pain and guilt to no one.
I should've told you that summer -
How I really felt to see you smile,
How the faint crease your forehead adorns,
Looks somehow just like a crown.
And how you, unknowingly,

Irked me out of my depravity.
But the meaningless instrument,
that men christen as heart,
Has no bottom to the abyss -
That failed longings conceive.
And hence, wordless, I thought,
That you would know my self,
And read me like your loved novel,
And find out all reasons why I smile.
Unrequited it is, that curse that -
Now has become my bane;
this emptiness bottomless rising,
from within to drown out my scream.
But would you yet hear someday
my voice calling out, in spirit?
Or would you still remain oblivious
To the world I had created,
In my dreams of the future?
Go on now, to that present,
that you lovingly chose for yourself,
You would deny my questions anyway.
But know I am here, still here,
for I have nowhere to go;
And I stand yet sometimes,
On the middle of that open road,
That took you away from me
To that far off land where -

My dawn is your midnight,
on the other side of existence.
But then I know now that,
You never gave it much thought.
I still have pictures from my childhood,
Of all the friendly picnics, and mirth,
From when I knew so little of the world,
I wish I had known then what I do now,
to be able to recognize those whims.
But you need not worry, my love,
I am like a mountain scarred,
Standing resolute and still;
And firmly this little belief I hold dear,
A lie that I parade as my truth;
I would like to say 'I am fine,
never been better before'.

9. Through the Sunset

The sun smiled a shade of amber,
Trees, rustling with the gentle wind,
Like the caress of distanced lovers –
Reunited, sighed in peace.

The amber orb crept lower,
Past the pine trees in the distance,
A raindrop caught the dying light
And sparkled like a star premature.

The dying star flitted through the canopy,
Upon a little spring it fell,
Like a divine muses' artist,
Trying to say goodbye.

With the final touch, a promise sown,
Of a fiery return on the horizon,
The artist and the muse retired,
With a patient smile to the speckled sky.

Their story will continue with the orb,
And countless verses shall be conceived,
When the new sun rises soft again,
And caresses its muse divine.

10. Sway

Where would you go in your dreams?
What would you see with eyes half-closed?
Will it be the fading fragrance of roses;
Or the wind blowing the petals away?

The moon hangs low as the world slumbers;
And the sentient stars keep a careful watch.
The sun will soon rise in our everblue sky;
And the shooting stars will melt away.

How would you then colour your dreams,
If not in shades of rainbows eternal?
Would you choose the everblack night,
Or the morning songbird's sway?

11. Paradox

I have roamed these roads before,
When the starlight up was dim.
Hand in hand two strangers walked,
Like scenes from within a dream.

Under the moonlight pale and dusty,
We voiced our fears and hopes.
When the west wind blew our way,
We held ourselves with paper ropes.

That kiss we shared so enchanting, as
Under the stairway she leaned in close,
My mind drifted to a pleasant sunset,
And the petals of a snowy rose.

A gypsy soul, a dreamer wild
She spoke of love and rain,
When the evening sun had gone
Her eyes reflected pain.

My love, my heart, my muse unearthly.
My delirious Winter equinox,
Her smile my drug, a fleeting fancy,
My beautiful solemn paradox.

12. Muerte del amor

I wandered a new road uncharted,
On a cold November's night;
Waiting for my beloved's arrival,
To save me from my plight;
Frost winds cruel but block my path,
Blowing fast with all their might.

She came in like a gentle breeze,
And left as a raging windstorm;
Knew not what she meant to me,
So conceded trying to conform;
I wondered shaken if she knew,
She was my precious home.

It seemed she'd had enough now,
Of our daydreams wrapped in red;
And as she ran so far a distance,
A cold in my heart did spread;
When the final goodbye was writ,
I lay broken and awake in bed.

Now we'll pretend it's over again,
We don't know our own names;
Some fires they blaze too bright,
Burning everything as games;
Others lost in vague translations,
Cannot rekindle their flames.

Some souls serene are meant to be,
Blessed by the glorious Jove;
Some break away like falling leaves,
Feelings deep down they shove;
Beware the cold and cruel heartache,
Behold, the tragic death of love.

13. Ode on an abditory

There was a ragged soul once so mellow,
That now wept away the silent nights;
Spending his years confined, confused,
Trying to take in all the midnight sights.

Alone in the twilights of his sadness,
Walls around him he placed anew;
Brick by brick he pieced them together,
Till the cracks left were bared few.

Sitting still in quiet drained reflections,
Never will he now feel that pain;
Along came but a little lost sparrow,
Went through the cracks again.

Flitting, fluttering round the walls up,
She sang a chirping, whistling song;
He gazed at her in silent amazement,
Her flight, his eyes mapping along.

That child of nature so pure and free,
Sang a joyous song of wind and rain;
The walls crumbling then came down,
Taking sadness all down the drain.

The sparrow free perched on his lap,
And filled his heart with joy profound;
He thus dared again to love and hope,
Writing anew another story astound.

He smiled, dancing from side to side,
With that morning songbird's sway;
He held her close, like a favourite rose,
In a childhood diary, tucked away.

She promised all the world in shades,
Of sunset red and midnight blue;
But as the dream and cloudscape ended,
Out his grasp, like a kite she flew.

Shattered hopes, a forever lost again,
The masks they now show undone;
But still he waits by the open window,
For his beloved's graceful slow return.

There was a ravaged soul alone, broken,
Who sighed away her tender memory;
Biding his slow time, writing, waiting,
Singing odes to his Winter abditory.

14. Thousand words

Tonight feels like thousand words,
Tales of dragons, solid gold swords;
Of angels with harps playing sly chords,
And raging feuds of seven warlords.

Silence slowly closes in,
From walls around me paper-thin,
"Hark" cries darkness from within,
Slithering deep beneath my skin.

Tonight I recant frayed stories anew,
Memoirs, memories beloved a few;
Of Sunsets cold as morning dew,
And secrets no one ever knew.

Quiet in mist's sonorous chimes,
Breaking rhythms of ancient rhymes,
Calling to eyes tumultuous times,
Raising scores of blood-cold crimes.

Tonight through the shifting sands of dreams,
Morpheus masks myriad muffled screams,
Night of Neverland starless seems,
Ruptured reality, shapeless seams.

The air abuzz with diaphanous chords,
Setting down the bloodied swords,
Dragon talons crusted on death lords,
Speak no more of a thousand words.

15. Ode on an older self

They told me it's been ages, since
They saw me paint on faded pages;
So, I gazed vacant hard and long,
To conceive yet another song.
Whence I met this teacher mine,
Who sought once to show a path divine;
And as she walked in the breeze,
An enchanting whiff did us then please;
But when we turned for answers few,
Like two kids up long past curfew –
I saw this ancient glow so bright,
Turning the jet-black sky alight.
This light was no man, nor a god,
But memoirs of roads that I had trod.
When I was young in days of yore,
I knew some things that ne'er were lore;
A secret only I knew then,
That escaped minds of many a men.
I turned again to seek the man,
But he'd strolled off without a plan;
And now his trail is lost in the dark,
No light can find him, no saviour's ark.

The memoirs but still illuminate –
The broken path that's in my fate.
I found in reflection's lofty shrine,
The shadow I sought, was only mine.
I knew then what I had to do,
To do, die, or bid adieu;
And so I picked my pen up then,
And wrote of love and pain and rain.
So watch me fill up one more page,
As I stand on this makeshift stage;
Under the returning evening songbird's sway,
And fold this sheet, and walk away.

16. Songs by the seashore

Moments pass by, then minutes, hours perhaps.
I stand motionless staring straight ahead,
Grains of sand shift beneath my feet
Like dreams, with receding waves.

The moon seems shy as it peeps from between clouds,
Does she not know I'm among her lovers many?
Waves serpentine are claimed back by the sea,
And I wonder if I should silently follow…
Looking away from the frothing fuming waves,
I turn my gaze to the clouds beyond the lighthouse…
Receding rain kissed my lips and bade goodbye,
Smiling, I whispered a long loved poem;
Lightning forked the sky as if enraged,
Like it knew not how to share love,
But even then it did not touch the waters.
Wavering waves stopped a moment, then continued
Lapping at my feet, calling me into a gentle embrace.
I wondered again if I should indulge their request;
Shaking my head I tucked my hand into my pockets,
Sighed, walked backwards and turned away…

Going back, I saw names in the sand wash away,
And thought how little I had done till now,
Before washing away, forgotten forever, then
Came home in silence, and began anew.

17. Lover

You know these walls these days they're always closing in?
I'm on my farthest stretch and I can't hear through the din.
But when you tell to me calm down, breathe out, breathe in,
I can't see the end, and don't know where to begin.

But you know these walls will always be here?
My soul struggling to break through,
And yet, look at me smile Sherry,
I finally wrote this song for you.

You know the dreams we drew out on nights like this,
When lights are dim, and shadows, bright?
Those nights now feel like dreams unseen,
I can't see the end, and don't know how to begin.

But you know the walls seem thicker now?
Breathless, trying to claw through.
And yet, hear me weep lover,
I really wrote this song for you.

You know all the ways I could say this,
I love you, I wish to make things right.
Is it really too late? Are you too far gone?
I can't begin, and this is the end?

Are the walls all now solid stone?
My voice can't break through?
Please hear me, my true Love,
I only sing this song for you.

You've said your goodbyes and made your peace
While all I have left are memories,
of us back then, of you and I.
I can't begin, and don't know how to end.

The walls are now solid iron,
My fists are bleeding rust.
But look at me lover,
I still wait right here for you.

18. Clouds of change

Yesterday I saw a cloud like you;
In the sky like birds you danced,
Across a pearly-white shore,
And I birthed a tale part-true.
This lonely tale, a brief recluse,
Was a world once made for two,
But in the end only one survived;
And the other, saw this through.

Yesterday I saw the sky crimson;
Today it's all white – blue.
I longed to escape this prison,
The heavens, I wished to subdue.

I tried to climb a mountain high,
To somehow reach the stars.
Grasping for a ghost in the sky;
Like faded old scars.

Today I see the castle no more,
The rainclouds have all gone;
And in the wake, just as before,
I stand here all alone.

Your dreams haunt me, tonight;
But they don't scare anymore.
Let ghosts stay where ghosts do,
You have your dreams, I mine too.
I make my stand upon this peak,
This mountain I have climbed;
I leave behind your distant shore,
My story I re-write.

19. Rainclouds and a stranger

I met a stranger tonight,
Who sang in verses old – of love long lost;
And the misery it had caused.
She was a wavering quivering soul,
Her voice frolicking like a waterfall,
Danced circles round your heart,
And left you astound in wonder.
She carried a world of hurt within herself;
From her words it always seemed.
For none but those who've been through hell,
Can sing such hymnal verses.

My warm stranger,
Are the rainclouds blocking your stars tonight?
It rained for me too, a few sennights ago;
No light ever shone through.
In a million words you've already heard before,
I could tell you it's going to be alright,
But it won't, and that's the truth.
Our demons never really give us up;

But we live with them somehow.
I wonder if you have sunny days,
Or all you see are clouds.

My perfect stranger,
It's cold tonight, after the rain.
I wonder if you still lie awake;
Or slumber in the arms of Dream.
In words I'd forsaken long ago,
I tried to sing a song for you,
No rhyme no reason you'll ever find here;
Just a bunch of words I had to say,
And two questions I had to ask;
Did you know rainclouds have silver linings?
Would you look for them with me?

20. I wrote you a letter

Last night, I wrote you a letter;
and today, I write you into poetry.
It has been a while since we last talked,
It has been a while since our lasts.

Did you know fireflies are not the only creatures
That glow in the deepest of dark?
Did you know I had it in me after all,
To drown you out, and speak up?

Yes, I speak to you, tonight, Sherry
But not in those old tongues.
This is something grander now,
This is me; my world of words!

Did you know I remember you still?
It's almost funny to think that
I never named someone in my poetry.
Firsts for everything, right?

I'm tired of chasing an impossible dream,
I'm tired of peeping through the hole in the wall.
I'm tired of trying to rhyme every line,
Poetry is supposed to be more than that right?

Right?
Sherry, it's been a while since I sang you a song,
And tonight, perhaps after ages long,
I tried to sing for you like no one's listening,
But I wondered if I should, and stopped.
I didn't want to anymore.
This was it.
My love,
I let you go.

21. Dancing demons, changed clouds

It has been four years now since –
We sang of dancing clouds and changing demons -
With a piece of our hearts untainted.
I wonder sometimes still,
Why are all my poems always about you?

Yesterday the sky was ablaze again,
And today the heavens are a cold steel grey.
All the world still rushes on,
But we have become a thing of the past.

Blue skies and grey clouds envelop my eyes today,
But they can no longer cuff their binds on me.
I have found my respite in this world of lies,
In the deep dark waters of art.

I miss the call of the sea, lulling, inviting,
And stormclouds passing us by,
Our skies will always change colours, I know
The sea will hypnotize us to dream.

The sea changes, and so does the sky;
A million miles now lay between us,
The clouds have all changed their shapes,
And the demons begin their dance.

The threads tying us together once,
Have all since disappeared unannounced,
We have moved onwards, but are we still the same?
My demons do not call for you anymore.

It has been four years now since –
Our songs and dance had once begun.
Our hearts are now tainted black.
I wonder in the end again –
Why are all my words for you?

22. In search of a place called home

The Sun blazes fiercely today,
even in the early hours of morning.
There used to be days when I felt
Like the world should stop spinning,
And yet here I sit, patiently waiting,
and hoping for a miracle.

There are days when I'm poetry,
There are days when I'm art.
There are days when I'm not myself,
When my troubles never part.

The Sun grows stronger every second,
The minutes slowly passing by;
There used to be days I spent lost,
Trying to find meaning of my self.
There used to be days when I spun words,
Immortalizing memories.

There are days I feel devoted,
There are days I feel proud,
There are days when the wild west wind,
chills me to my bones.

The Sun will set on the only sky we've ever known,
and like sunrises, perhaps our paths will cross again.
Like this river we will keep dancing, chuckling,
and bear brave, victorious smiles.
There used to be days when I felt helpless,
Now, I feel undaunted, invincible.

There are days that I love you,
There are days that I believe,
There are days when I forget you,
and breathe sighs of relief.

23. My Shooting Star

I saw a shooting star yesternight,
as I lay upon my lonely roof,
but forgot to make a wish;
lost in my own old musings,
of a world of yours and mine;
Where hopes and dreams flourish.

The shooting star burnt itself out,
in the sky and in my memories;
and my dreams continued.
The wish I forgot to make,
was for you and I to be us,
but lost, they were subdued.

The dying Sun does little to ease my pains,
I feel like the world I knew is all but gone,
And all that remains is fuming burning ash.

I squint up at the everblack sky for stars,
But for them to sparkle through for us,
The moons shines a bit too brightly tonight.

I fear repeating the same ideas and words
That I have used for ages endless.
but melancholiacs do not work that way.

How does a poet then express himself,
If not in words he has always known? And,
sing of the only love he has ever known?

I see no stars tonight,
The moon is all too bright.
My mind dances to a sunset we shared,
As if we witnessed a world ending.
I cannot wish upon that star,
I see no stars tonight.

So, instead I weave words,
To preserve that memory.
In the form of you and I,
As yet another 'eternity' presents itself.
My Meraki, my lost love's labour,
Did you know shooting stars never stay,
yet shine the brightest in the sky?

24. Why writers bleed

Ask me not if I know why -
writers bleed and a poet dreams;
Ask me instead then why they love
to create a world of their own.
It's not for fortune, nor for fame;
It's not a side-quest, nor a game.
for memories made, promises sown,
over paper their pens they move
creating oceans, lakes, rivers and streams;
full of hopes, of dreams under the sky.

Ask me not if I know why –
they sing always of love and pain,
It's their world, their only recluse,
the only home they've ever had.
So wonder awhile, in their stories stay;
and find out what they want to say.
Once done, you might call us mad,
we may disagree but have no excuse,
we'll have nothing to lose or gain,
but in earnest again we will try.

So, ask me your questions now –
the things you really want to know.
I will promise you a thousand verses,
and in them you will find yourself.
This is our home, our world of words,
where titans fight with bloodied swords.
This is where eternity presents itself,
with magic, music, whispers, curses,
to ends of this earth we'll together go,
if only your feet, and will would allow.

I ask you now with all my might,
to lay the bloodied swords down,
the battle is again lost, and won.
so, come along away with me,
We will dance with dragons in the sky,
and you will finally know why –
Writers smile and a poet is always free.
so, come with me, and together as one,
I will show you a world of words my own,
and in the end, we will become starlight!

25. Drown

In commemoration of this special day,
A fickle hand glides over my instruments of creation,
Tonight, they dance and create only for you.
You gave me piece of your azure wild ocean,
without ever knowing what oceans mean to me.
The waves call me back home relentlessly,
and you brought a piece of home back to me.
I took it in wonder, treasured it a sennight,
gratitude demanded I give you something in return,
So, I give you this piece of my soul, forged just for you;
a dormant ocean inside a seashell split in two;
I would swim with you if I could, but I would drown.

Oceans are in a lot of ways like people,
They wash over us and pull the sand under our feet,
and yet when they go, we stand stronger somehow.
So take this piece of ocean I crafted for you,
let it adorn your skin like a jewel priceless,
or let it sit with a million others that came before,
With this last verse conceived, I bid my goodbye,
and dive to drown in this ocean I have dreamt up.
Remember, still waters like this often run deep,

and rivers of magic lie dormant in your heart,
they all lead to this ocean of endless starlight.
Flow, my Love. Do not drown.

26. Yours, Mine.

There are nights when the world ceases to exist for me in entirety;
Tonight will be such a night as I gaze onto the sky in search of stars.
I wonder if you dream of me sometimes; because my sweet love,
in my dreams you are resplendent as the sun shining on our horizon.
In my dreams you and I fly to ends of sensations, to the ends of earth.
In my dreams, we conjure up the most intricate, elaborate of mysteries,
In my dreams we paint the skies with a million diamonds, together.
We sing and dance to the songs we have always known the words to;
We lay under moonlight, and this night never bids goodbye.
It is amazing how even the shortest distance in the world
can feel like the longest, harshest road you ever trod upon.
In my dreams that distance takes two heartbeats to cross -
mine, and yours.

There are nights when my mind leaves me alone with my senses,
Tonight is such a night as I wonder what keeps pulling me to you.
I wonder if these dreams will end someday; because, my Love,
In my dreams I have counted the deaths of a thousand stars.
In my dreams I have seen roses offered to gods of seas in vain.
In my dreams we dance to songs I write for you, and you sing.
In my dreams I show you my entire world of endless love.
We soar and glide with clouds at our feet, masters of the sky.
We laugh in this world of infinite choices, you never bid goodbye.
There is nothing left for me to give to you anymore,
So I give you this last piece of who I once used to be,
This little garden of words and memories, a paradise -
Yours, and mine.

27. The Climb

I went on a journey -
Through the crevices of my mind,
To find out where, what demons lurked;
To figure out what, why they said to me,
In strangest whispering tongues,
Driving me insane.

The journey, when it started first,
Was a dark and dreary broken road,
Where nightmares reigned and fears trod;
Where demons' cries made blood run cold;
and seeking, hoping, I travelled on,
and met a merry word-magician.

I asked her what her name was,
But that she could not tell me then;
so instead she gestured at a distance -
to where a mountain stood proud, tall.
I turned to her again for answers,
she just smiled and said, 'Climb.'

I was on this journey alone, when she came and showed me the way;
so towards the mountain I traversed on, and asked her if she would stay.

I recanted tales mine old to tell her all of -
my midnight cries and daylight woes;
when bled and bled I for memories lost,
Till broken, shaken, I reached a doorway,
and walked through this dreamscape mine,
and found her along my lonely way.

The magician then spun my tales,
and showed me things I had missed out;
I pondered on my past decisions,
all the roads I walked so far;
and in that duet of reflections,
I found my self, myself.

The mountain stood in front of me now,
And I gazed at it in worry, weary of the task,
The magician cast a spell, with words of light,
then slowly turned to me and whispered -
'There is a pool of endless power within you,
an entire world of creation; so, Climb.'

I fell, bruised, broken, a couple of times, but I climbed up - scratched and clawed my way to the top; she climbed with me.

As we now stand on this mountaintop
I see the world and make time stop
One journey's end, another begins,
and the magician lets go of the reins.
The journey is yet to end, an endless track,
but my words once lost find their way back.

The magician stands awhile beside me,
and asks where I go now and what I see -
Hills on my horizon, rivers cutting my roads,
Where else do I go now, except onwards?
I turn to thank the magician but she disappears,
so, alone again, I cross the world's frontiers.

The journey now is still long and hard,
but I have within me this little bard.
That sings wayward pleasing rhymes.
and creates worlds with clever schemes.
so let this then be known far and wide -
I wished to rise; so, I climbed.

I am anything but a perfect being; but with light in my heart, and magical music in my soul; I walk, I write, I climb.

28. Almost, always.

We push and pull like yin and yang,
dancing round the flames ablaze.
We fear getting burnt and back away,
coming close to being one,
almost, always.

We dance around in circles close,
chasing our own hopes and fears.
We smile from a distance and wait,
our fingers longing to intertwine,
almost, always.

We know all our demons by name,
we have danced with them too.
But when we talk of our darkness,
we shy away from answers,
almost, always.

In the days, all through the night,
your visions haunt me now.
I remember the thousand days

that we spent together -
almost, always.

We laugh together like kids,
at some silly midnight musing.
We look at each other in awe,
our lips inches away from a kiss,
almost, always.

The push and pull has ended now,
the dance and fire burnt out.
we are scorched to ashes, dust,
never coming close again,
always, almost.

Our circles part a million miles,
as we walk our separate ways.
Our smiles are not for us anymore,
our fingers will intertwine,
always, almost.

Our demons now have all but won,
the blacks and whites grow grey.
In the darkness of our solitary minds,
the answers we seek come to us,
always, almost.

The nights are cold and days long,
all your visions blurred and dim.
the thousand words and worlds,
will be spoken of again,
always, almost.

We smile now in our separate worlds,
our musings, wishes have changed.
Looking for ourselves in other people,
our paths will cross again like -
always, almost.

29. Dreams on a full moon night

In the cold winter of November winds,
I spent a night on a rooftop with just my thoughts -
Of the clouds rolling overhead, and the stars,
Waiting for me to begin counting.

In the season of mists, a memory rewinds -
And wraps my heart up in knots.
I wonder if this night is really ours;
the Moon is full, exhaustion mounting.

I hear the soothing lull of sleep
calling me to lands of dreams;
so I pack my bags and bid adieu
and drift off slow, then dive in deep.

I hope and pray this night does not end,
and when I do, my dream begins.

At first, I see an endless expanse -
a dark pit of downward spirals.

I fell as though through my own will,
and came out on a sandy shore.
The sky grew darker as I gazed around,
soaking in a new sapphire horizon.
I wondered where I was - in vain,
there were no souls to be seen.
The ground below begged my attention,
my feet in sand by a restless sea.

Alone with the waves of this world,
I sat awhile in wonder why -
sunsets always make me smile sadly.
I looked around, and slowly made my way
to sheer cliffs on one steep side;
I walked on till I reached the edge,
and saw the Sun devoured by the sea.
I wondered why I see beauty in melancholy,
and on the precipice of that unnamed cliff,
I sat alone, and thought of you and me.

Footsteps distant drifts to my weary ears,
I turn to investigate the sound's source;
and amazed, I see you running towards me.
You cross the waters, climb up the cliff,
and panting, stand in front of me.
Not a spirit, and nor a spectre,
you are a resounding reality.

Hand in hand, we walk again;
and build a fire in a cliffside cave,
this new universe now we see.

The night moves slowly,
unknown predators outside lurk,
but we are protected by our flames.
We name this world, "The Frairie Lands"
and claim it with our creation's fire, as our own.
As the predators go away declaring us masters,
we see a million stars reflected on an empty sea.
Countless stories end, our universe unwinds.
we still lay near the fire, in our home,
by the lonely restless starlit sea.

This is where our paradise begins,
the place where all our nightmares end.

On the plains of Frairie dancing,
our naked feet run on blades of grass.
And then on shores of the starlit sea,
we watch the tides of time turning.
So let us now end this little lore,
but stay awhile more I pray,
and then say goodbye, for today,
To our little home by the sea.

My rooftop dreams end no more,
the night now all but drifts away,
and come dawning light, Love, I say
homewards bound we'll be.

30. Eden, goodbye.

This is a true story,
A slightly strange one at that.
Of love, heartbreaks, and dreams.
Of a wordsmith walking alone,
and the love he once had lost.
How he then reclaimed his craft,
and built a universe out of nothing,
and here, made his dreams a reality.

You must all know for sure,
That the wordsmith is plain old me.
I created a world within my mind,
to keep my love alive and well.
This world of dreams and stories,
was once meant for both of us;
But when she went I was left alone,
to sing odes in search of her.

This story begins with darkness cold,
and inches towards the warm light.
Our stars don't shine on us anymore,
so I throw diamond dust in the sky,

and hope to God it sticks.
and as the dust now slowly settles,
I find a myriad score of words, stories
begging me to spill them all.

So then, what is left now,
but to dance with the Muses' memories?
They draw up intricate deliriums for me,
and hastily, I pen them all for you.
The distance between us grows longer
with every passing moment fleeting,
but in my stories we are never apart,
in my poems you are here with me.

There is a castle on a snowy mountain,
where a silver dragon guards old books.
There is a grove that glows in moonlight,
and strange creatures call it home.
There is a little house by side of a lake,
in the heart of a forest of magic.
with all these little places together,
we built our land of dreams.

There is a warlock with a dragon familiar,
who lives by a riverside alone.
There is a towering prison by a cliff,
where damsels in distress are locked.

There is a portal to another world,
within a forest old and brown.
With all these tales, we chose to name it -
our home, our paradise, our Eden.

Ever since you went away,
these stories are all I have.
So I dream up more intricate worlds,
endless poems for you I write.
With a little wish of loving again,
somewhere down our roads;
I preserve pieces of you and I, of us,
inside this dreamscape we once called ours.

Your skies would never be the same,
if chance makes us meet again.
Would you recognize a man you once knew
if you saw him someday after ages?
Would you remember his views and ways,
Remember how his smile used to reach his eyes?
Now, only empty dark brown pits pull you in,
to nothingness.

In our Eden, we were immortals,
The world of men at our feet;
but you couldn't stay for long,
my mistakes pushed you away.

So, alone here, my eternal muse,
A strange thought but comes to mind:
The opposite of immortality is oblivion,
not mortality; don't you see?
The castle's broken, all books burnt out.
The grove cut down, all creatures dead.
The warlock alone, his dragon has flown.
the damsels ran away, into the portal.
Only our house by the lake remains.
The deliriums are gone; the dreamscape all explored.
Nine muses, ninety poems. How many more?
My demons have now all been sealed. So, nevermore!

I tried to make this poem about something else,
but in the end it ended up being yours, again.
After all these years, I have stopped asking
Why my awakening came with our demise,
Instead I free the words trapped within me,
and write you into cursive immortality.
My poems, prayers and promises,
all for you, always for you.

All poems writ, all prayers made,
All promises turned into stories -
the tales have all been ended.
I am at my wits end to say more,
So here this story will have to end.

I let go of my immortality here,
and now, welcome oblivion;
My Eden, I bid goodbye.

Curtain Call

Dear Reader,

If you have reached this far, I thank you from the bottom of my heart for being a part of this journey. Ending credits are supposed to be dramatic, they are supposed to make an impact on you, so people get hooked to you. But you know what? I didn't really want to do any of that. I am simply writing to you, my beloved reader, because writers and poets are not writers and poets without their readers. It is you that fulfils our purpose in this world for us, when you decide to take a journey through our hearts, minds, and souls; and to put it quite plainly, I would never have had the courage to publish a book if it hadn't been for the people who read and kept on telling me to go forward with this. Thank you, all of you, for making this happen for me.

Too sappy? I'll try and tone it down. There's no fancy wordplay or a rhyme scheme to be found here. It's just me, writing you a letter, and letting you know that no matter who you are, if you read through these pages, I love you with all my heart and soul. I have always loved writing and people always encouraged me to write more and more, and it broke my heart to give it up for two entire years. It wasn't that I didn't write, I couldn't write. And the thing about unexplored doorways are: you never really know if you'll ever be able to go back once they slam shut behind you. In a way, this is me trying to push open that closed door. For now, I see a faint crack between the doors, and through that little crack my poems come pouring out.

Like all good things, I end this with hope. I hope you liked at least one poem here. For me, every single one of them has a special memory or a thought behind it. This is how I preserve memories and people: through poetry. There is something so beautifully tragic about bleeding your heart out on a piece of paper for all the world to see. I hope you have people in your life who inspire you to attempt impossible things, I hope there are people who make you feel like you are flying, and I hope you have someone to bring you back to your reality occasionally, too. I hope you have people to care about, and people who care about you. Because at the end of the day, we are made up of bits and pieces of all the people we have ever loved. These poems are, in fact, some of my pieces.

There are so many stories I want to share with you now, so many amazing places full of magic and life. But for now, I'm tired. If you would allow me, maybe another time?

With love, hope and endless gratitude,

Yours,
Utsav

About The Author

Utsav Jain, 25; has been writing for the better part of a decade, ever since he realized a person can express their thoughts and feelings to their fullest extent onto paper for all the world to see. Born in the culturally diverse atmosphere of Kolkata, he had been exposed to a wide range of artforms from a very young age.

He started writing back in 2011; the words and thoughts of a thousand dreamers before him began whispering in his head one day; and have never stopped since. A communications manager by day, an artist and writer by night; Utsav has always enjoyed creating; be it poetry, stories, or pieces of the numerous artforms he practices. Utsav dreams to reach out to the people of the world and paint their world with his creations. He invites you to sit back and, through his words, let him take you away to enchanting foreign lands full of romance and heartbreak, fantasies and nightmares, love, and life.

Utsav lives in Ahmedabad. Apart from writing, he enjoys cycling, long walks by rivers, exploring new places, getting lost in music, cooking, and creating art pieces.

9 798885 217682

Printed by Libri Plureos GmbH in Hamburg, Germany